LiV

D1594943

A RAINBOW OF
Smoothie Bowls

100 Wholesome
and Vibrant Blended Creations

LEIGH WEINGUS

Ulysses Press

Published in the U.S. by:
Ulysses Press
P.O. Box 3440
Berkeley, CA 94703
www.ulyssespress.com

ISBN13: 978-1-61243-6050
Library of Congress Control Number: 2016934499

Printed in China by Everbest through Four Colour Print Group
10 9 8 7 6 5 4 3 2 1

Acquisitions editor: Casie Vogel
Project editor: Kourtney Joy
Managing editor: Claire Chun
Editor: Renee Rutledge
Proofreader: Lauren Harrison
Front cover and interior design: whatdesign@whatweb.com
Layout: Jake Flaherty
Photographs: © Celine Rahman

Distributed by Publishers Group West

For Brenna

CONTENTS

INTRODUCTION

When I first started telling people I was writing a book about smoothie bowls, they were a little confused. Sure, they'd heard about the green smoothie trend. Toss some kale, almond milk, and a banana in a blender, and voila! You're basically eating salad for breakfast, except it's sweet, delicious, and drinkable.

Smoothie bowls, on the other hand, are a more difficult concept to grasp. What kind of smoothie is best consumed with a spoon rather than a straw? That doesn't seem normal.

But, after all these months, I'd like to think I've mastered the art of explaining (and marketing) the magic of a smoothie bowl. Think cereal and milk, granola and yogurt, or any other delicious breakfast combination in a bowl. Except, in this case, you've got a smoothie instead of milk or yogurt, and nuts, seeds, and fruit instead of cereal and granola. Smoothie bowls are also very colorful and pretty, making them even more appealing.

Don't get me wrong: I love smoothies on their own and have done so since before they were cool (or so I like to think). While a basic smoothie can be healthy, delicious, and filling, I'm of the opinion that it's hard to be entirely satisfied when you drink your breakfast. Once you add nuts, fruit, seeds, and chocolate, though, your smoothie starts to feel a lot more like a meal.

A BRIEF HISTORY OF THE SMOOTHIE BOWL

Although I'd like to take credit for the rise of the smoothie bowl, that would be far from the truth. My first experience with a smoothie bowl was all the way back in 2007 at a tiny cafe nestled cozily in the mountains of Santa Cruz, California. It was called Cafe Brazil, and it had an odd yet popular menu item: an acai bowl (that's pronounced ah-sigh-ee, for anyone who's wondering).

Acai bowls were the most popular item on the menu, and the waiters were quick to school me on this antioxidant-packed berry that grew in the rain forest. It was colorful, sweet, cool, and refreshing. It was not to be missed!

This granola and strawberry–topped bowl did not disappoint: It was cool, refreshing, sweet, and crunchy. I was on board.

A few years later, acai bowls started to blow up. The trendiest restaurants in New York, Los Angeles, and San Francisco offered acai bowls for brunch. I went to Hawaii in 2013, and acai bowls were everywhere. They were nutritious and tasty, sure, but there was something else: They were really pretty.

Naturally, when people started photographing their food and posting it on social media (myself included), acai bowls became a popular item on Instagram feeds everywhere.

Even better, it seemed that people were branching out from the classic acai bowl and experimenting with other colorful frozen fruit, vegetable, nut, and seed combinations that were even prettier than acai bowls. For lack of a more creative term, they were called smoothie bowls.

MY PERSONAL HISTORY WITH THE SMOOTHIE BOWL

You know those people who don't wake up hungry? Yeah, I'm not one of them. The moment my alarm goes off, I don't even hit snooze because I'm famished.

For that reason, breakfast has always been especially important to me. I've gone through tons of phases with it, too. I spent years eating sugar-loaded "energy" bars because people told me they were good for me and other years eating bowls of sugary cereal that left me exhausted and grouchy all day long.

On top of being a smoothie bowl enthusiast, I'm also a health editor and yoga instructor. That being said, it should come as no surprise that I'm someone who places a lot of importance on feeling her best.

When it became clear that my Luna Bar and Honey Nut Cheerios habit was becoming detrimental to how I felt all day, I quickly realized something had to change when it came to my breakfast routine. I experimented with oatmeal, which made me feel pretty good and kept me full for hours, and although a little bit bland, I didn't mind having plain Greek yogurt for breakfast either.

Still, something was missing, and I loved the idea of jam-packing fruits, vegetables, protein, fiber, and healthy fat into my breakfast. With smoothie shops popping up all over New York City, I finally discovered a way to do just that. But I was getting a little tired of forking over 10 dollars every time I wanted to sip on some green deliciousness.

So one summer I begged my parents to buy me a high-speed blender as an "early birthday present" (this was in June, my birthday isn't until November), and they agreed to go in on it with me.

Just like that, my life was changed. Overnight, I became the girl who was bringing mason jars full of green goop to work much to the disgust of my coworkers, who didn't believe me when I told them how delicious my green breakfast was.

Soon enough I was posting my colorful concoctions on Instagram, where I found people who actually seemed to be interested in my newfound breakfast obsession. Three years later, a crunchy, fruity, slightly sweet smoothie bowl is still my favorite way to start the day.

WHEN SMOOTHIE BOWLS GET UNHEALTHY

The smoothie bowl trend is a great one, and I firmly believe that there's no better breakfast option. But before you fire up your blender, it's worth noting that a smoothie bowl can get unhealthy *real* fast if you're not careful.

For example, a few years ago I was using orange juice instead of almond milk as a base for my bowls, and I was starving and exhausted an hour after breakfast. I had no idea what was going on until I took a closer look at the ingredients on my orange juice carton.

I had somehow missed the fact that most orange juice brands have a ton of added sugar. The fruit in your smoothie has enough natural sugar on its own, so adding juice, sweetened almond milk, or fruit-flavored yogurt into the mix is a recipe for a sugar crash.

While not every smoothie bowl in this book is crazy healthy (just wait until you get to the Halloween bowl), every recipe calls for unsweetened almond milk or the unsweetened nut milk of your choice. If you don't want a giant sugar bomb for breakfast, this is the best liquid base for your smoothie. If you'd rather have dairy in your smoothie, unsweetened Greek yogurt is a great option as well.

In the cases where smoothies could use some extra sweetness—this is surprisingly necessary in recipes that call for cocoa, as cocoa on its own is pretty bitter—bananas, dates, cinnamon, and small amounts of honey and maple syrup are great natural ways to sweeten up your bowls.

I'm not going to bore you with the many reasons why breakfast is the most important meal of the day, but I will say that a super-sugary breakfast without protein or fat will leave you feeling tired and craving more sugar throughout the day.

Although some of these recipes have a good amount of calories, the calories are generally made up of nuts, avocados, and coconut, which are packed with good fat, protein, and fiber and will keep you full all day long. According to research, a caloric (but healthy) breakfast will actually lead you to consume fewer calories throughout the day.

BUT AREN'T SMOOTHIE BOWLS EXPENSIVE AND TIME-CONSUMING?

Another concern people have brought to me as I've worked to spread the word on smoothie bowls is that they seem like an expensive and time-consuming breakfast option. Why spend the money and all that time in the morning when you can just dump a pack of oatmeal into a bowl, add hot water, and call it a day?

Listen, I'm all about the easy, cheap breakfast option. But I also think that with the right equipment and solid grocery store knowledge, smoothie bowls are just that. Plus, they have way more nutrients in them than that pathetic envelope of apple cinnamon–flavored oatmeal.

Nuts and seeds are super affordable when you buy in bulk or even in smaller amounts online. As for fruit, it *can* be really expensive if you do it wrong. I've purchased enough tiny cartons of blueberries and raspberries that cost $6.99 to know that.

But, if you buy in season, fruit is actually really inexpensive (and tastes a lot better, as an added bonus). If those prices are still too steep, spend a few more minutes in the frozen fruit aisle of your favorite grocery store. After an hour of thawing, you'll barely be able to taste the difference.

As for the time-consuming aspect of it, I agree that putting together an elaborate bowl on a weekday morning might be a little unrealistic. Instead, make your smoothie the night before, store it in a mason jar, and have your toppings ready to go in a zip-top plastic bag for the next morning. It might not look as pretty, but it will taste just as good.

You can even go so far as to make a week's worth of smoothie bases on Sunday night. As long as they're stored securely in a mason jar, they should keep through Friday.

IF YOU'RE DOING IT FOR THE SAKE OF INSTAGRAM

If you do have a few extra minutes to spare for presentation, it's important to keep a few things in mind.

If your recipe calls for heavier toppings like nuts, seeds, or bulky fruits, you want your smoothie base to be able to hold them. Adding frozen bananas, nut butters, yogurt (dairy or not), or almond meal can be a great way to add some bulk to your base.

If that's not really your thing, simply slip your bowl in the freezer for half an hour or so after blending up your base. This will firm it up enough to hold your toppings, give you time to take a nice picture of it if you so desire (hey, there's no shame in enjoying a whole lot of Instagram likes), and you can relish it after a few minutes of thawing.

In my experience, smoothies look much better when photographed in natural light, so if a photo opportunity is what you're looking for, find it when you have a decent amount of sunlight to work with.

Having colorful bowls helps, too. If you don't feel like investing in more bowls, smoothie bowls are just as delicious and beautiful when served in coffee mugs and wine glasses. It's all in the creativity.

HOW TO USE THIS BOOK

Although I probably *could* eat a smoothie bowl every morning, I don't. Sometimes I'm craving oatmeal, chia seed pudding, pancakes, or French toast for breakfast.

So although smoothies are a fantastic way to incorporate vegetables, fruits, and healthy fats into your breakfast, I'm hardly asking you to ditch other delicious breakfast options and spend every morning with your blender.

Instead, try having a smoothie bowl a few times a week. Do you feel better on the days when you've got spinach, kale, bananas, and almond butter before 9 a.m.? If so, maybe it's worth it to up your smoothie bowl intake to five a week. If not, more power to you—I'm personally a huge fan of unsweetened oatmeal with a little bit of banana, so go crazy.

And while I'll be beyond flattered if you use all of my recipes in your future smoothie bowl endeavors, I also encourage you to experiment with different combinations of bases and toppings.

Maybe where I suggest a banana, for example, you'd prefer a scoop of peanut butter. A smoothie bowl is a form of creative (and delicious) expression, so don't be afraid to explore a range of ingredients and flavors.

Happy blending!

INGREDIENTS AND EQUIPMENT

For some people, smoothie bowls are an exotic art form. While I'm all for expressing myself with nuts, seeds, fruits, and veggies, some of the ingredients included in smoothie bowls are really hard to find or just really expensive.

For that reason, I'm skipping pitaya fruit (also known as dragon fruit), spirulina, and edible flowers and other pretty yet odd ingredients you may have seen on your Instagram feed.

All of the ingredients I recommend are easy to find at your local supermarket or grocery store, so get ready to stock up.

STAPLES

If you're planning on blending your way through this entire book, start by stocking your pantry with these staples.

- Bananas (to use immediately and to freeze)
- Frozen blueberries
- Frozen strawberries
- Frozen raspberries
- Dried goji berries
- Cacao nibs
- Dark chocolate chips
- Your favorite granola
- Chia seeds
- Pumpkin seeds
- Hazelnuts
- Cinnamon
- Vanilla
- Unsweetened shredded coconut
- Almond butter or the nut butter of your choice
- Unsweetened almond milk or the nut milk of your choice. Coconut, almond, and cashew milk are great options.

The other ingredients you'll find in these recipes are fresh fruits and vegetables, so you can purchase them at your local grocery store or farmer's market as needed.

All of the recipes in this book use 10 ingredients or fewer, so if you're already stocked up on the basics, your grocery list will be pretty small.

One final note: Unless frozen fruit is specified, the recipe calls for fresh fruit or vegetables.

EQUIPMENT

The most important thing you need for your smoothie bowls is a blender. A high-speed blender like a Vitamix or Blendtec is the ideal way to go, but if you're not up for spending that much money, a more inexpensive blender like an Oster or

NutriBullet will work just fine. Just know that blending up your bases may be more time-consuming and frustrating (trust me, I've been there).

Other than that, just make sure you have measuring cups, measuring spoons, and a pretty bowl to pour your smoothie in.

A note on toppings: Although I include measurements for toppings, other than the light bowls (page 115) that include a calorie count, they're more suggestions than anything, so you know what to aim for. You don't need to waste all your time perfectly measuring an eighth cup of blueberries every single time!

SPRING
Bowls

As the weather warms up and apricots and oranges start to come into season, there's no better way to celebrate the new season than with a smoothie bowl. Plus, spring means vibrant colors, new beginnings, and some fun holidays. The perfect time to get creative.

EASTER BASKET BOWL

Don't freak out, there aren't any hard-boiled eggs involved here—just pretty spring colors and flavors, and maybe even some chocolate.

Base

½ cup frozen mango

1 banana

1 cup almond milk

1 teaspoon vanilla

Toppings

¼ cup blueberries

⅛ cup grapes

1 strawberry, sliced

⅛ cup granola

INSTRUCTIONS

Make your base. Add mango, banana, almond milk, and vanilla to blender, and blend until smooth. Transfer to a bowl.

Add your toppings. Line bowl with blueberries, grapes, strawberries, and granola.

. . . .

VARIATION If you're in the mood for something a bit more sinful, make this bowl all about chocolate by swapping out one or two of the fruit toppings for:

- Chocolate chips
- Dark chocolate bar
- Cadbury Creme Egg

Tip: If you want to avoid weighing the whole bowl down, chop the Cadbury Creme Egg up and evenly distribute across surface.

. . . .

BLUEBERRY KIWI BOWL

Base

1 frozen banana

½ cup blueberries

1 cup almond milk

Toppings

½ kiwi, sliced into half moons

¼ cup blueberries

⅛ cup sliced raspberries

INSTRUCTIONS

Make your base. Add banana, blueberries, and almond milk to blender, and blend until smooth. Transfer to a bowl.

Add your toppings. Add kiwi slices to center and line border of bowl with raspberries on one side and blueberries on the other.

. . . .

VARIATION For a more tropical twist on this bowl, swap the blueberries and raspberries with these:

- 1 tablespoon shredded unsweetened coconut
- ½ cup sliced pineapple

. . . .

STRAWBERRY LEMONADE BOWL

Strawberry smoothies are delicious and all, but it's always fun to mix it up. If you've ever had strawberry lemonade, you already know strawberries and lemons make a good combination. So you can't really go wrong here.

Base

1 banana

1 cup frozen strawberries

1 lemon, juiced

1 cup almond milk

Toppings

⅛ cup blueberries

⅛ cup blackberries

1 strawberry, sliced

⅛ cup pineapple chunks

1 teaspoon shredded unsweetened coconut

INSTRUCTIONS

Make your base. Add banana, strawberries, lemon juice, and almond milk to blender, and blend until smooth. Transfer to a bowl.

Add your toppings. Line bowl with blueberries, blackberries, strawberry slices, and pineapple chunks, and sprinkle shredded coconut on top.

TIP: Although this isn't a requirement (you can always use your hands), I highly suggest investing in a citrus squeezer. You get less mess and a whole lot more juice out of the deal.

PINEAPPLE KIWI BOWL

When it's almost summer but not quite, you're thinking long and hard about summer things, like tropical drinks. So get a head start on summer with this pineapple kiwi bowl.

Base

1 banana

1 cup frozen pineapple

1 cup almond milk

Toppings

⅛ cup pineapple chunks

⅛ cup blueberries

½ kiwi, sliced into half-inch-thick rounds

½ banana, sliced into half-inch-thick rounds

INSTRUCTIONS

Make your base. Add banana, pineapple, and almond milk to blender, and blend until smooth. Transfer to a bowl.

Add your toppings. Line bowl with pineapple chunks, blueberries, kiwi, and banana slices.

TIP: For added flavor (and because kiwis are everywhere), try adding kiwi to the base. Can't have too many kiwis!

NUTTY AVOCADO RASPBERRY BOWL

Avocado automatically makes any smoothie bowl creamier (and more delicious). Once you add a spoonful of nut butter, you'll have energy all day long.

Base

½ avocado

1 cup raspberries

1 cup almond milk

Toppings

¼ banana, sliced into half-inch-thick rounds

⅛ cup granola

⅛ cup blueberries

⅛ cup raspberries

1 tablespoon almond butter

INSTRUCTIONS

Make your base. Add avocado, raspberries, and almond milk to blender, and blend until smooth. Transfer to a bowl.

Add your toppings. Line one side of bowl with banana slices and granola and the other with blueberries and raspberries. Add the almond butter to center.

TIP: Store the other half of the avocado with the pit still in it in an airtight container. This will help you avoid the dreaded brown avocado, so you can toss it in another smoothie or have it with lunch.

KIWI BANANA BOWL

Kiwi is the best spring fruit. Eating it on its own is great, and eating it on top of a creamy smoothie is even better.

Base

1 frozen banana

1 cup almond milk

1 teaspoon vanilla

Toppings

1 kiwi, sliced into rounds

1 teaspoon shredded unsweetened coconut

INSTRUCTIONS

Make your base. Add frozen banana, almond milk, and vanilla to blender, and blend until smooth. Transfer to a bowl.

Add your toppings. Stack sliced kiwi on top of base and sprinkle coconut on top.

TIP: Never be afraid to freeze your fruit, especially your browning bananas. Because almost all of my smoothies are banana based, I have a giant container full of frozen bananas in my freezer at all times. And the riper they are, the sweeter their flavor.

So if any of your fruit starts to look a little too ripe and you're not ready to use it, please don't throw it away! Freezing it retains its flavor and nutrition, so just toss it in a freezer bag and use it for a future smoothie.

MANGO KIWI BOWL

Mango and kiwi make the ideal flavor and color combination. When you throw blueberries and raspberries into the mix, you've got a perfect rainbow smoothie bowl.

Base

1 cup frozen mango

1 cup almond milk

Toppings

handful of raspberries

handful of blueberries

1 kiwi, sliced into half moons

INSTRUCTIONS

Make your base. Add frozen mango and almond milk to blender, and blend until smooth. Transfer to a bowl.

Add your toppings. Line bowl with raspberries and blueberries, and add kiwi to center.

TIP: If you can't find frozen mango, frozen pineapple is a great option for this as well. As an added bonus, pineapple happens to be cheaper!

ST. PADDY'S DAY BOWL

If you're a fan of Saint Patrick's Day, green beer, and Shamrock Shakes but want to make your day a little healthier, give this extremely delicious (and nutritious) St. Paddy's Day bowl a try. You can smugly drink it while everyone else is loading up on less healthy treats.

Base

1 frozen banana

1 cup almond milk

½ cup spinach

Toppings

2 clementines, peeled and separated into slices

¼ cup green grapes

½ banana, sliced into half-inch-thick rounds

INSTRUCTIONS

Make your base. Add banana, almond milk, and spinach to blender, and blend until smooth. Transfer to a bowl.

Add your toppings. Line bowl with clementines, grapes, and sliced banana.

. . . .

VARIATION You can also try these toppings:

- ⅛ cup dried apricots
- ½ kiwi, sliced
- ¼ cup shredded unsweetened coconut

. . . .

APRICOT STRAWBERRY BOWL

Apricots are a fruit I always forget about until spring rolls around, and then I can't stop eating them. So naturally I freeze them, blend them up for my smoothies, and then pile *more* on top. Adding a strawberry really ties the whole thing together.

Base

1 banana

4 frozen pitted apricots

1 cup almond milk

Toppings

½ cup dried apricots

1 strawberry

INSTRUCTIONS

Make your base. Add banana, apricots, and almond milk to blender, and blend until smooth. Transfer to a bowl.

Add your toppings. Top with dried apricots and add strawberry to center.

VARIATION Mix things up with these toppings:

- ⅛ cup blackberries
- ¼ cup chopped watermelon
- 3 strawberries

TIP: If you can't find them pitted, buy fresh apricots, take the pits out, and freeze them.

VERY BERRY MANGO BOWL

For me, spring is all about loading up on the berries I didn't have much access to during the freezing cold winter months, which is why I absolutely love heaping them on top of my smoothie bowls.

Base

1 banana

½ cup frozen mango

1 cup almond milk

Toppings

⅛ cup blueberries

⅛ cup blackberries

⅛ cup raspberries

2 strawberries, sliced

INSTRUCTIONS

Make your base. Add banana, mango and almond milk to blender, and blend until smooth. Transfer to a bowl.

Add your toppings. Heap blueberries, blackberries, raspberries, and sliced strawberries on top in no particular order.

VARIATION Turn this into a melon bowl! Try these toppings:

- ⅛ cup cantaloupe
- ⅛ cup watermelon
- ⅛ cup honeydew
- 1 teaspoon honey, drizzled on top

CARROT BLUEBERRY GRANOLA BOWL

Let's just get this out of the way: This combination sounds super weird. Trust me, though—once you try it, you'll never go back.

Base

1 frozen banana

1 cup finely chopped carrots

1 cup almond milk

Toppings

¼ cup blueberries

¼ cup granola

1 tablespoon shredded unsweetened coconut

INSTRUCTIONS

Make your base. Add banana, carrots, and almond milk to blender, and blend until smooth. Transfer to a bowl.

Add your toppings. Top with blueberries and granola, and sprinkle coconut on top.

TIP: Always read your granola labels. A lot of granolas are packed with sugar and butter, and sometimes that's the last thing you want on top of an already sweet bowl. Whether it's low calorie, low sugar or low fat that you're looking for, make sure to scan the ingredients list before buying so you can make an informed decision.

SUMMER
Bowls

It's summertime, and the living's easy. Stock your pantry with berries and other colorful fruits and get ready to eat smoothie bowls all summer long. After all, do you really want to eat oatmeal on 80-degree mornings?

CREAMY MANGO GOJI BOWL

The awesome thing about working with mango is that it's a naturally creamy fruit. So when almond milk and bananas get involved, you basically have mango ice cream.

Base

1 banana

1½ cups frozen mango

1 cup almond milk

Toppings

⅛ cup dried goji berries

1 tablespoon shredded unsweetened coconut

INSTRUCTIONS

Make your base. Add banana, frozen mango, and almond milk to blender, and blend until smooth. Transfer to a bowl.

Add your toppings. Line bowl with goji berries and sprinkle shredded coconut in center.

VARIATION Try something different with these toppings:

- 1 teaspoon hemp seeds
- 1 teaspoon chia seeds
- ⅛ cup dried goji berries
- ⅛ cup fresh mango

PIÑA COLADA BOWL

Who wouldn't want to start their day with a healthy version of a piña colada? You can add alcohol to this one if you want, but I don't recommend having it for breakfast.

Base

1 banana

1 cup frozen pineapple chunks

1 cup unsweetened coconut milk

Toppings

⅛ cup fresh pineapple chunks

⅛ cup shredded unsweetened coconut

INSTRUCTIONS

Make your base. Add banana, pineapple chunks, and coconut milk to blender, and blend until smooth. Transfer to a bowl.

Add your toppings. Line border of bowl with pineapple chunks and sprinkle coconut evenly on top.

VARIATION If regular old coconut milk that comes in a box and tastes a lot like almond milk isn't doing it for you, up the creaminess by using a can of light coconut milk instead.

BASIC BLUEBERRY BOWL

This one is about as basic as it gets, and I mean that in a good way. It doesn't have many ingredients, it's healthy, and it tastes great.

Base

½ banana

2 cups frozen blueberries

1 cup almond milk

Toppings

½ banana, sliced into half-inch-thick rounds

⅛ cup slivered almonds

drizzle of honey

INSTRUCTIONS

Make your base. Add banana, frozen blueberries, and almond milk to blender, and blend until smooth. Transfer to a bowl.

Add your toppings. Line bowl with banana slices and add slivered almonds to center. Drizzle honey on top for a bit of added sweetness.

TIP: To beef up this bowl a bit, add half an avocado to the base. If you want a little more sweetness, toss a date in there and prepare to taste the difference in flavor and texture.

RASPBERRY RAINBOW BOWL

With berries seriously in season, it's hard to find an excuse *not* to pile berries on top of your smoothie bowl. This recipe allows you to do just that.

Base

1 ½ cups frozen raspberries

1 cup almond milk

Toppings

¼ banana, sliced into half-inch-thick rounds

⅛ cup blueberries

⅛ cup raspberries

1 teaspoon shredded unsweetened coconut

1 basil leaf

INSTRUCTIONS

Make your base. Add raspberries and almond milk to blender, and blend until smooth. Transfer to a bowl.

Add your toppings. Top with ribbons of banana slices, blueberries, raspberries, shredded coconut, and basil.

. . . .

VARIATION Taste the rainbow with these toppings:

- 1 mint leaf
- ⅛ cup mango
- ⅛ cup raspberries
- ⅛ cup cashews

. . . .

FOURTH OF JULY BOWL

Want to be patriotic *and* healthy this summer? Whip up this Fourth of July bowl.

Base

1 frozen banana

1 cup almond milk

Toppings

½ banana, sliced into half-inch-thick rounds

⅛ cup blueberries

⅛ cup raspberries

INSTRUCTIONS

Make your base. Add banana and almond milk to blender, and blend until smooth. Transfer to a bowl.

Add your toppings. Line bowl with bananas slices, blueberries, and raspberries. Add one banana slice to center and stick an American flag on top. (This is optional, of course, but it's fun!)

· ·

VARIATION Try these equally patriotic toppings:

- 1 tablespoon dried goji berries
- 1 tablespoon dark chocolate chips
- ⅛ cup blueberries
- 1 tablespoon shredded unsweetened coconut

· ·

CHERRY PIE BOWL

Cherry pie is pretty good. Cherry pie smoothie bowls are even better. The colorful toppings make this one of the prettiest smoothie bowls ever, and the basil adds a funky, fresh taste.

Base

1 banana

1 cup frozen cherries

1 cup almond milk

1 teaspoon vanilla

Toppings

⅛ cup sliced strawberries

⅛ cup blueberries

⅛ cup granola

3 shredded basil leaves

INSTRUCTIONS

Make your base. Add banana, cherries, almond milk, and vanilla to blender, and blend until smooth. Transfer to a bowl.

Add your toppings. Top with lines of strawberries, blueberries, granola, and shredded basil leaves.

TIP: If you have trouble sleeping, this smoothie bowl might be better consumed at night. According to some research, cherries help you sleep.

CHOCOLATE-COVERED STRAWBERRY BOWL

Okay, so this bowl doesn't actually include chocolate-covered strawberries. But it tastes just as good as a chocolate-covered strawberry, mostly because there are actual bars of chocolate in it.

Base

1 banana

1 cup frozen blueberries

1 cup almond milk

Toppings

¼ (1.55-ounce) dark chocolate bar, broken up into four pieces

2 strawberries

INSTRUCTIONS

Make your base. Add banana, strawberries, and almond milk to blender, and blend until smooth. Transfer to a bowl.

Add your toppings. Submerge chocolate bar pieces in base and top with strawberries.

. . . .

VARIATION Try these toppings instead:

- ⅛ cup chocolate chips
- 1 strawberry
- ⅛ cup blueberries

. . . .

PEACH COBBLER BOWL

When juicy peaches are in season, you have to take advantage of them. Up your peach game by layering this peach smoothie between strips of granola and topping it with summer berries.

Base

1 banana

1 cup frozen peaches

1 cup almond milk

Toppings

½ cup granola

⅛ cup raspberries

INSTRUCTIONS

Make your base. Add banana, peaches, and almond milk to blender, and blend until smooth. Transfer to a bowl.

Add your toppings. Layer as follows in a small clear bowl: peach smoothie, then granola, then peach smoothie. Top with granola and raspberries.

· ·

VARIATION If peaches aren't really your thing but you love their vibrant color, try using frozen apricots or frozen pineapple for the base instead.

· ·

MANGO BANANA BLUEBERRY BOWL

The great thing about summer is that berries are seriously on sale, so you don't have to pay $5.99 for that tiny carton of blueberries. I load up on fresh blueberries every chance I get in the summer months, and I especially love dumping them on top of my smoothies. Add raspberries and you've got every color of the rainbow.

Base

1 banana

1 cup frozen mango

1 cup almond milk

Toppings

¼ cup blueberries

¼ cup raspberries

½ banana, sliced

INSTRUCTIONS

Make your base. Add banana, mango, and almond milk to blender, and blend until smooth. Transfer to a bowl.

Add your toppings. Heap blueberries and raspberries next to each other on one side of bowl, and line the opposite side with sliced banana.

PINEAPPLE BLACKBERRY BOWL

Pineapple tastes like summer, as do blackberries. The combination of blackberries and pineapple is sweet, sour, and extremely summery.

Base

1 banana

1 cup frozen pineapple

1 cup almond milk

Toppings

¼ cup blackberries

⅛ cup raspberries

1 teaspoon hemp seeds

1 teaspoon chia seeds

INSTRUCTIONS

Make your base. Add banana, pineapple, and almond milk to blender, and blend until smooth. Transfer to a bowl.

Add your toppings. Line border with blackberries, raspberries, hemp seeds, and chia seeds.

VARIATION If you want this exact same flavor without any toppings, add the blackberries to the base and blend the whole thing up. This is a perfect on-the-go breakfast.

AVOCADO SPINACH BOWL

This is basically the greenest smoothie bowl in the world. It's also flat-out delicious and has a super-satisfying crunch.

Base

1 frozen banana

1 cup spinach

½ avocado

1 cup almond milk

Toppings

1 tablespoon shredded unsweetened coconut

1 tablespoon cacao nibs

1 tablespoon dried goji berries

⅛ cup granola

INSTRUCTIONS

Make your base. Add banana, spinach, avocado, and almond milk to blender, and blend until smooth. Transfer to a bowl.

Add your toppings. Add ribbons of coconut, cacao nibs, goji berries, and granola.

- -

VARIATION To sweeten up this base a bit, try adding any or all of these ingredients:

- honey
- maple syrup
- 2 dates

- -

FALL
Bowls

Believe it or not, a lot of fall vegetables make excellent smoothie bases. Think pumpkin and sweet potato. Sound weird? Once you add cinnamon, I promise you'll be in smoothie heaven.

BUTTERNUT SQUASH RASPBERRY BOWL

I first started tossing butternut squash into smoothies when I realized I didn't love it on its own. So I tried boiling it and blending it up, and I loved it. A butternut squash smoothie bowl is the perfect fall treat.

Base

1 cup frozen butternut squash

1 frozen banana

1 cup almond milk

1 teaspoon maple syrup

Toppings

⅛ cup raspberries

1 tablespoon cacao nibs

⅛ cup pumpkin seeds

INSTRUCTIONS

Cut butternut squash into 1-inch cubes and toss into a large pot of boiling water. Boil until squash is cooked through. Let cool for half an hour before tossing in the freezer for an hour minimum. If they're still not frozen, let sit for another hour.

Make your base. Add butternut squash, banana, almond milk, and maple syrup to blender, and blend until smooth. Transfer to a bowl.

Add your toppings. Line bowl with raspberries and cacao nibs, and sprinkle pumpkin seeds in center.

TIP: If you hate wasting food and love delicious treats, try roasting your butternut squash seeds with a bit of cinnamon. You can sprinkle them on top of your smoothie bowl for some crunch or eat them on their own.

PEAR BERRY BOWL

Because pears are so sweet, they taste great with berries, which tend to be on the more tart side. Pumpkin seeds add a little more fall and a whole lot more crunch.

Base

1 banana

1 cup almond milk

1 cup frozen pear cubes

Toppings

½ pear

½ banana

⅛ cup raspberries

⅛ cup blueberries

⅛ cup pumpkin seeds

INSTRUCTIONS

Make your base. Add banana, almond milk, and pear cubes to blender, and blend until smooth. Transfer to a bowl.

Add your toppings. Line one side of bowl with pear and the other with banana. Add raspberries, blueberries, and pumpkin seeds to center.

. . . .

VARIATION Also try these toppings:

- ½ banana, sliced into half-inch-thick rounds
- 1 tablespoon cacao nibs
- 1 teaspoon shredded unsweetened coconut
- ⅛ cup pomegranate seeds

. . . .

HALLOWEEN BOWL

The base of this one is simple and healthy. The rest definitely isn't. But it's really, really delicious. You can afford to splurge once a year!

Base

1 frozen banana

1 cup almond milk

1 teaspoon vanilla

Toppings

¼ cup M&M's

4 green grapes

⅛ cup chocolate chips

1 Snickers bar, broken into ¼-inch chunks

INSTRUCTIONS

Make your base. Add frozen banana, almond milk, and vanilla to blender, and blend until smooth. Transfer to a bowl.

Add your toppings. Pile M&M's, grapes, chocolate chips, and Snickers bar chunks on top.

VARIATION If you don't consider a bowl covered with candy a smoothie bowl, I don't blame you. Try these toppings instead:

- 1 orange, peeled and broken up into slices
- 4 Medjool dates
- 4 green grapes

APPLE, PEANUT BUTTER, AND MAPLE BOWL

Apple picking is one of my favorite fall activities, but I always pick way too many and end up with about 22 pounds of apples. There are only so many apple pies a person can make! Luckily, that perfect apple and peanut butter combination also tastes awesome in smoothie form.

Base

1 large apple, cut into chunks

1 frozen banana

1 cup almond milk

Toppings

½ apple, sliced thinly

1 tablespoon peanut butter

1 cinnamon stick

1 teaspoon maple syrup

INSTRUCTIONS

Make your base. Add apple, banana, and almond milk to blender, and blend until smooth. Transfer to a bowl.

Add your toppings. Add thin apple slices to side of bowl, and add scoop of peanut butter to center. Place cinnamon stick on side of bowl and drizzle maple syrup on top.

TIP: If peanut butter isn't really your thing or you want your bowl to be a little healthier, try using almond butter instead. The combination is just as delicious, and you'll get more nutrients out of the deal.

CINNAMON OAT BOWL

Nothing screams fall quite like cinnamon, and this tastes exactly like a fresh-baked cinnamon roll, except that it's healthy. Doesn't get much better than that.

Base

½ cup oats, cooked and chilled

½ banana

1 cup almond milk

1 teaspoon ground cinnamon

1 teaspoon vanilla

Toppings

⅛ cup raspberries

⅛ cup blackberries

1 tablespoon almond butter

½ banana, sliced

1 teaspoon ground cinnamon

INSTRUCTIONS

Make your base. Add oats, banana, almond milk, cinnamon, and vanilla to blender, and blend until smooth. Transfer to a bowl.

Add your toppings. Pile raspberries, blackberries, almond butter, and banana on top. Sprinkle cinnamon on toppings.

PUMPKIN PIE BOWL

Base

1 frozen banana

½ cup pumpkin puree

1 cup almond milk

Toppings

¼ cup raspberries

¼ cup granola

2 cinnamon sticks

1 teaspoon ground cinnamon

INSTRUCTIONS

Make your base. Add banana, pumpkin, and almond milk to blender, and blend until smooth. Transfer to a bowl.

Add your toppings. Top with raspberries, granola, and cinnamon sticks, and sprinkle cinnamon on top.

TIP: Try tossing a small handful of dates into your blender. This will add a naturally sweet, smooth taste to your smoothie and make it taste a lot more like dessert.

BLUEBERRY CHOCOLATE CHIP APPLE CHIA BOWL

There is nothing better than eating dessert for breakfast, especially when it's healthy and won't lead to a sugar crash before lunch. Tossing chia seeds in there will add crunch and keep you full for hours.

Base

1 frozen banana

1 cup blueberries

1 teaspoon unsweetened cocoa powder

1 cup almond milk

Toppings

½ apple, sliced into chunks

⅛ cup raspberries

1 tablespoon chocolate chips

1 teaspoon chia seeds

1 teaspoon maple syrup

INSTRUCTIONS

Make your base. Add banana, blueberries, cocoa, and almond milk to blender, and blend until smooth. Transfer to a bowl.

Add your toppings. Top with apple chunks, raspberries, chocolate chips, and chia seeds. Drizzle with maple syrup.

. . . .

VARIATION Although chia seeds are the most mainstream of the seeds out there, if you want some variety or you're not a huge fan, try experimenting with:

- hemp seeds
- sunflower seeds (without the shells)
- sesame seeds
- flaxseeds

. . . .

APPLE PIE BOWL

Wouldn't it be great if apple pie wasn't packed with sugar? This one is basically Thanksgiving in a smoothie bowl—without the guilt.

Base

1 frozen banana

1 apple, sliced into chunks

1 cup almond milk

Toppings

1 handful raspberries

½ apple, sliced

⅛ cup granola

⅛ cup pecans

⅛ cup chocolate chips

INSTRUCTIONS

Make your base. Add banana, apple, and almond milk to blender, and blend until smooth. Transfer to a bowl.

Add your toppings. Heap raspberries, apple, granola, pecans, and chocolate chips on top.

TIP: If you don't feel like this bowl is complete without whipped cream, buy a can of coconut cream (it's a lot less sinful than it sounds, as most cans don't have added sugar). Whip it with a spoon for about 30 seconds and add it to your smoothie bowl.

SWEET POTATO SAGE BOWL

When you need a break from berries and you're craving something unique and flavorful, this is the perfect option for fall.

Base

1 sweet potato

⅛ cup fresh sage

1 cup almond milk

1 teaspoon ground cinnamon

Toppings

1 banana, sliced into ½-inch-thick rounds

1 teaspoon ground cinnamon

1 teaspoon maple syrup

INSTRUCTIONS

Bake sweet potato for 45 minutes (chopping up and boiling works as well), and freeze.

Make your base. Once frozen, add frozen sweet potato, sage, almond milk, and cinnamon to blender, and blend until smooth. Transfer to a bowl.

Add your toppings. Evenly distribute banana slices across surface, and sprinkle cinnamon and maple syrup on top.

· ·

VARIATION Try these toppings:

- ⅛ cup pecans
- 1 teaspoon ground nutmeg
- 1 teaspoon ground cinnamon
- 1 teaspoon honey
- 2 Medjool dates

· ·

SUPER CINNAMON BOWL

Cinnamon is great for a lot of reasons. Aside from being delicious, cinnamon has a ton of unexpected health benefits. Cinnamon can help treat muscle spasms and nausea and may even help fight cancer. I love sprinkling it on top of my oatmeal, pancakes, and smoothies because it adds a natural sweetness without the sugar.

Base

1 frozen banana

1 cup almond milk

1 tablespoon almond butter

1 teaspoon ground cinnamon

Toppings

¼ cup raspberries

3 cinnamon sticks

1 teaspoon ground cinnamon

1 teaspoon maple syrup

INSTRUCTIONS

Make your base. Add banana, almond milk, almond butter, and cinnamon to blender, and blend until smooth. Transfer to a bowl.

Add your toppings. Line bowl with raspberries and add cinnamon sticks to center. Sprinkle with cinnamon and drizzle maple syrup on top.

CHOCOLATE RASPBERRY BOWL

It looks and tastes like dessert, but it's actually healthy. Need I say more?

Base

1 ½ frozen bananas

1 cup almond milk

1 tablespoon unsweetened cocoa powder

1 teaspoon maple syrup

Toppings

⅛ cup raspberries

1 tablespoon cacao nibs

⅛ cup pecans

INSTRUCTIONS

Make your base. Add frozen bananas, almond milk, cocoa powder, and maple syrup to blender, and blend until smooth. Transfer to a bowl.

Add your toppings. Line bowl with raspberries, cacao nibs, and pecans.

TIP: To add flavor and bulk to this bowl, toss in ¼ cup of chilled pumpkin puree to the base. Now you've got a pumpkin chocolate bowl, and it's arguably more delicious.

WINTER
Bowls

Winter may not seem like the best season for smoothie bowls, but with a season full of heavy foods it can be nice to start your morning on a fresh, light note. Plus, winter fruits like blood oranges make for delicious and beautiful smoothie bowl toppings.

MANGO BLOOD ORANGE BOWL

There's no doubt about it: Blood oranges are dramatic-looking, which is why they're the perfect pop of color when you're going with a basic green smoothie. They also happen to be delicious and one of the best parts of winter.

Base

1 banana

1 cup frozen mango

1 cup almond milk

1 cup spinach

Toppings

¼ cup granola

1 blood orange slice, cut in a circle

INSTRUCTIONS

Make your base. Add banana, mango, almond milk, and spinach to blender, and blend until smooth. Transfer to a bowl.

Line bowl with granola and place blood orange slice in the center.

. . . .

VARIATION For a option, try these toppings:

- ⅛ cup granola
- 1 clementine, peeled and broken up into slices
- 1 blood orange, peeled and broken up into slices

. . . .

CLEMENTINE SUNSHINE SMOOTHIE BOWL

Just as the name implies, this is basically a bowl of sunshine. It takes a lot of peeling, but the result is worth it—especially because the amount of clementines on top will make you forget that your bowl is green.

Base

1 frozen banana

2 clementines, peeled and frozen

1 cup almond milk

1 cup spinach

Toppings

4 clementines, peeled and broken into slices

1/8 cup raspberries

1/8 cup blueberries

1 basil leaf

INSTRUCTIONS

Make your base. Add banana, clementines, almond milk, and spinach to blender, and blend until smooth. Transfer to a bowl.

Add your toppings. Line bowl with clementines (this should take up the majority of the bowl), and add raspberries, blueberries, and basil to center.

. . . .

VARIATION Mix it up with these toppings:

- 2 clementines, peeled and broken into slices
- 2 blood oranges, peeled and broken into slices
- 1/8 cup blackberries
- 1 mint leaf

. . . .

NUTELLA SMOOTHIE BOWL

Winter makes me think of hiding out with Netflix and, more often than not, a jar of Nutella. If you're a fan of the taste but could do without some of the unhealthy aspects of that little jar of goodness, whip up this smoothie bowl.

Base

1 frozen banana

1 cup almond milk

⅛ cup hazelnuts

1 teaspoon unsweetened cocoa powder

Toppings

¼ cup chocolate chips

¼ cup hazelnuts

INSTRUCTIONS

Make your base. Add banana, almond milk, hazelnuts, and cocoa powder to blender, and blend until smooth. Transfer to a bowl.

Add your toppings. Add chocolate chips to one side of the bowl and hazelnuts to the other.

TIP: If you have a food processor, try blending up your hazelnuts with a little bit of cinnamon and making hazelnut butter. You can add this to the base or pour it on top.

CLEMENTINE MINT SMOOTHIE BOWL

One great thing about winter is that clementines are in season. They're great as an afternoon snack and arguably better blended up in a smoothie. Plus, the color helps you forget that it's so dreary outside. It can be tough to get these bowls thick enough to hold their toppings, so freeze your banana and clementine slices.

Base

4 frozen peeled and separated clementines

1 frozen banana

1 cup almond milk

Toppings

1 clementine, peeled and broken into slices

3 shredded mint leaves

1 tablespoon dried goji berries

1 teaspoon unsweetened shredded unsweetened coconut

INSTRUCTIONS

Make your base. Add clementines, banana, and almond milk to blender, and blend until smooth. Transfer to a bowl.

Add your toppings. Line bowl with clementine slices, then add mint leaves, goji berries, and coconut to center.

· ·

VARIATION If you want to make this one even more citrusy, try using orange juice as a base instead of almond milk. It does get more sugary this way, but it's also super refreshing.

· ·

HOLIDAY BOWL

Okay, so this one isn't made up of winter fruits—but it does look (and taste!) exactly like the holiday season. Cinnamon is good for that.

Base

1 cup frozen cherries

1 cup almond milk

1 teaspoon ground cinnamon

Toppings

⅛ cup raspberries

¼ banana, sliced into ½-inch-thick rounds

⅛ cup chocolate chips

4 green grapes

INSTRUCTIONS

Make your base. Add cherries, almond milk, and cinnamon to blender, and blend until smooth. Transfer to a bowl.

Add your toppings. Add raspberries, banana slices, chocolate chips, and grapes to surface.

TIP: I am not at all opposed to putting candy on top of smoothie bowls. If you love candy canes, there's no shame in crushing one up and piling it on top of your smoothie bowl.

BLOOD ORANGE GRAPE BOWL

This bowl is nutty, citrusy, and sweet. It's the perfect winter breakfast, snack, or dessert.

Base

1 ½ frozen bananas

1 cup almond milk

1 teaspoon vanilla

Toppings

6 blood orange slices

⅛ cup blueberries

⅛ cup pecans

⅛ cup green grapes

⅛ cup raspberries

INSTRUCTIONS

Make your base. Add bananas, almond milk, and vanilla to blender, and blend until smooth. Transfer to a bowl.

Add your toppings. Line bowl with blood orange slices, blueberries, and pecans. Add grapes and raspberries to center.

FUN FACT: On top of all the regular benefits that regular oranges have (like vitamin C and folic acid), blood oranges have something in them called anthocyanins, which are also found in blueberries. Although anthocyanins haven't been studied extensively, they are thought to protect against a variety of diseases.

GRAPEFRUIT GREEN BOWL

They can be bitter, sure, but grapefruits are packed with vitamin C (exactly what you need to ward off those winter colds). And when you add a little sweetness, they're absolutely delicious.

Base

1 frozen deseeded grapefruit

1 frozen banana

2 cups spinach

1 tablespoon honey

½ cup almond flour milk

Toppings

¼ cup pomegranate seeds

⅛ cup granola

1 teaspoon honey

INSTRUCTIONS

Make your base. Add grapefruit, banana, spinach, honey, and almond milk to blender. Blend until smooth, and transfer to a bowl.

Add your toppings. Line bowl with pomegranate seeds and evenly distribute granola on top. Drizzle with honey.

TIP: To make this bowl even healthier, try adding a cup of kale. This will add vitamins and thicken your bowl up a bit.

CREAMY CHOCOLATE PEPPERMINT BOWL

If winter makes you think of chocolate and peppermint, you're not alone. 'Tis the season! So why not get your fix in a healthier way?

Base

1 banana

1 tablespoon unsweetened cocoa powder

1 cup almond milk

1 tablespoon maple syrup

1 teaspoon vanilla

Toppings

8 mint leaves

⅛ cup raspberries

⅛ cup chocolate chips

INSTRUCTIONS

Make your base. Add banana, cocoa powder, almond milk, maple syrup, and vanilla to blender, and blend until smooth. Transfer to a bowl.

Line bowl with mint leaves and raspberries and add a pile of chocolate chips to center.

TIP: If you want an extra burst of energy, try adding half a teaspoon of matcha to this base. It won't alter the taste dramatically, and you'll get some extra health benefits and long-lasting energy. I don't know about you, but I almost always need that on cold winter mornings.

SWEET POTATO RASPBERRY BOWL

If the thought of blending up frozen sweet potatoes weirds you out, I don't blame you. But when I was craving a smoothie one morning and only had sweet potatoes on hand, I tried this out and never went back. It requires some prep work, but it tastes just like pumpkin pie and is surprisingly refreshing.

Base

1 cup frozen sweet potato chunks

1 banana

1 cup almond milk

Toppings

handful of raspberries

1 tablespoon shredded unsweetened coconut

1 teaspoon cacao nibs

INSTRUCTIONS

Peel and chop sweet potatoes and add to a large pot of boiling water until cooked through. Let cool for half an hour before tossing in the freezer for 1 hour minimum. If they're still not frozen, let sit for another hour.

Make your base. Add frozen sweet potatoes, banana, and almond milk to blender, and blend until smooth. Transfer to a bowl.

Add your toppings. Line bowl with raspberries and add shredded coconut to center. Sprinkle cacao nibs on top.

TIP: Boiling your sweet potatoes is one way to do it, but you can just as easily bake them in the oven for an hour at 400°F, or even roast them with a little olive oil and brown sugar on top.

POMEGRANATE PERSIMMON BOWL

Pomegranates and persimmons are beautiful, sweet, delicious fruits that happen to be available everywhere in wintertime. Both make colorful smoothie toppings, and pomegranate seeds are perfectly tart, while persimmon slices are super sweet. You can't lose with this one.

Base

1 cup frozen strawberries

1 cup almond milk

1 tablespoon almond butter

Toppings

1 round fuyu persimmon slice (preferably from center of fruit)

½ cup pomegranate seeds

INSTRUCTIONS

Make your base. Add strawberries, almond milk, and almond butter to blender, and blend until smooth. Transfer to a bowl.

Add your toppings. Add persimmon slice to center and cover surrounding surface with pomegranate seeds.

TIP: If you have leftover pomegranate seeds, toss them in your blender with the base ingredients for a bolder taste and color.

PEPPERMINT MOCHA BOWL

If you're one of those people who loves a seasonal Starbucks drink, this is the smoothie bowl for you. It tastes a lot like a Peppermint Mocha, except it's not packed with sugar and hard-to-pronounce ingredients.

Base

1 frozen banana

¼ cup brewed coffee, chilled

1 cup almond milk

1 teaspoon maple syrup

Toppings

⅛ cup dark chocolate chips

1 tablespoon unsweetened whipped coconut cream

4 mint leaves

INSTRUCTIONS

Make your base. Add banana, coffee, almond milk, and maple syrup to blender, and blend until smooth. Transfer to a bowl.

Add your toppings. Top with dark chocolate chips, whipped coconut cream, and mint leaves.

TIP: Although coconut cream is delicious, because this entire bowl is so healthy it won't hurt to use a little whipped cream on this one if you're dying for some sugar.

EVERGREEN
Bowls

Even when your favorite fruits and veggies aren't in season, you can usually find a good amount of them frozen and get a taste of whatever season you're craving. Plus, some fruits are easy to find fresh in grocery stores year round. So when you don't feel like trekking to the farmer's market or are burning out on sweet potatoes and blood oranges in the colder months, try blending up one of these.

ENERGIZING RASPBERRY CHIA BOWL

Chia seeds are awesome. They're perfectly crunchy, help with digestion, and keep you full until lunch. Add some raspberries (which are packed with fiber) and almond butter (full of protein and good fat), and you'll be set for the day.

Base

1 cup frozen raspberries

1 banana

1 cup almond milk

Toppings

⅛ cup grapes

½ cup fresh raspberries

1 tablespoon chia seeds

1 tablespoon almond butter

INSTRUCTIONS

Make your base. Add raspberries, banana, and almond milk to blender, and blend until smooth. Transfer to a bowl.

Line bowl with grapes and raspberries. Spread chia seeds evenly across base and add spoonful of almond butter to center.

. . . .

VARIATION Try these toppings instead:

- ⅛ cup hemp seeds
- 1 tablespoon cashew butter
- ⅛ cup blueberries
- ⅛ cup raspberries

. . . .

MINT CHOCOLATE CHIP BOWL

Is there anything more satisfying than digging into a big bowl of mint chocolate chip ice cream? Not in my opinion. While I would love to eat mint chocolate chip ice cream for breakfast, all that sugar first thing in the morning is a recipe for a sugar crash, not to mention way too many calories. This is the perfect alternative.

Base

1 frozen banana

1 cup almond milk

small handful of mint leaves

1 cup spinach

1 teaspoon unsweetened cocoa powder

Toppings

⅓ cup chocolate chips

small handful of mint leaves

⅛ cup raspberries

⅛ cup blueberries

INSTRUCTIONS

Make your base. Add banana, almond milk, mint leaves, spinach, and cocoa to blender, and blend until smooth. Transfer to a bowl.

Add your toppings. Evenly distribute chocolate chips, mint leaves, raspberries, and blueberries on top.

FUN FACT: Aside from being delicious, mint is great for digestion and "cleansing the palate"—which is why chewing gum after a meal and brushing your teeth before bed leaves your mouth feeling fresh and neutral.

CHOCOLATE MANGO NUT BOWL

Have you ever tried combining mango with chocolate? If you haven't, now's your chance. The creamy mango base topped with cashews, chocolate, and raspberries makes this bowl super decadent.

Base

1 cup frozen mango

1 cup almond milk

1 teaspoon almond butter

Toppings

½ (1.55-ounce) bar dark chocolate

⅛ cup cashews

small handful of raspberries

INSTRUCTIONS

Make your base. Add mango, almond milk, and almond butter to blender, and blend until smooth. Transfer to a bowl.

Add your toppings. Break chocolate bar into a few pieces and scatter on top along with cashews and raspberries.

TIP: Research has shown that people who eat dark chocolate on a regular basis are actually happier and healthier than people who don't. Be cautious when checking out your ingredients, though: A healthy chocolate bar is 85 percent cocoa and has less than 10 grams of sugar per serving.

BLUEBERRY EVERYTHING BOWL

Sometimes you just want to let loose, and this blueberry everything bowl is basically a party disguised as a smoothie bowl. No rows, no rules—just scatter your toppings as you'd like and enjoy.

Base

1 cup frozen blueberries

1 banana

1 cup almond milk

Toppings

⅛ cup blueberries

⅛ cup raspberries

1 teaspoon cacao nibs

1 tablespoon pumpkin seeds

1 teaspoon shredded unsweetened coconut

INSTRUCTIONS

Make your base. Add frozen blueberries, banana, and almond milk to blender, and blend until smooth. Transfer to a bowl.

Add your toppings. Evenly—or unevenly, your call—spread blueberries, raspberries, cacao nibs, pumpkin seeds, and coconut across surface.

- -

VARIATION For a sweeter, crunchier alternative of this bowl, try these toppings:

- 1 tablespoon chocolate chips
- ⅛ cup dried blueberries
- ⅛ cup dried raspberries
- ⅛ cup granola
- ½ banana, sliced into ½-inch-thick rounds

- -

RASPBERRY FIG BOWL

Figs aren't always easy to get year round, but dried figs are. And they're an excellent, sweet smoothie topper. I personally think their color complements red berries well, but you can also try this topping combination with a blueberry bowl. This base is banana-free for a richer color.

Base

1 cup frozen raspberries

1 cup almond milk

Toppings

½ banana, sliced into ½-inch-thick rounds

⅛ cup blueberries

¼ cup dried figs, sliced in half

INSTRUCTIONS

Make your base. Add raspberries and almond milk to blender, and blend until smooth. Transfer to a bowl.

Add your toppings. Line bowl with banana slices, blueberries, and dried figs.

VARIATION Every so often it can be impossible to find figs, dried or otherwise. Lining this bowl with dates gives it a bit of a different texture, but it's just as delicious.

MATCHA VANILLA BOWL

Matcha is great for a lot of things—drinking on its own, adding to baked goods, and blending into smoothies. Not only does this powdered green tea have the prettiest green color ever, but it's full of health benefits like antioxidants and an amino acid called L-theanine, which gives you a feeling of calm alertness. On top of that, it's delicious.

Base

1 frozen banana

1 cup almond milk

¼ teaspoon vanilla

1 teaspoon matcha

Toppings

⅛ cup raspberries

1 tablespoon cacao nibs

1 teaspoon chia seeds

1 tablespoon shredded unsweetened coconut

INSTRUCTIONS

Make your base. Add frozen banana, almond milk, vanilla, and matcha to blender, and blend until smooth. Transfer to a bowl.

Add your toppings. Scatter raspberries, cacao nibs, chia seeds, and shredded coconut evenly across bowl's surface.

· ·

VARIATION If you want an earthier taste, try using hemp milk in this one. I personally think it pairs perfectly with matcha.

· ·

STRAWBERRY CHOCOLATE CHIP BOWL

It doesn't get much more decadent than this. Strawberries, bananas, chocolate chips...yep, this one is really tasty.

Base

1 banana

1 cup frozen strawberries

1 cup almond milk

Toppings

½ banana, sliced into ½-inch-thick rounds

⅛ cup blueberries

⅛ cup raspberries

⅛ cup chocolate chips

INSTRUCTIONS

Make your base. Add banana, strawberries, and almond milk to blender, and blend until smooth. Transfer to a bowl.

Add your toppings. Add lines of banana slices, blueberries, and raspberries to center. Line border of bowl with chocolate chips.

. . . .

VARIATION For a richer alternative on this bowl, try these toppings:

- ⅛ cup mango
- ½ (1.55-ounce) dark chocolate bar, broken into pieces
- ⅛ cup blackberries
- 1 tablespoon shredded unsweetened coconut

. . . .

SUPER-RED STRAWBERRY BOWL

I'm all about mixing up colors, but sometimes it's nice to have just one color to work with. In this case, it's red. Red is dramatic *and* delicious.

Base

1 cup frozen strawberries

1 frozen banana

1 cup almond milk

Toppings

⅛ cup raspberries

1 tablespoon dried goji berries

INSTRUCTIONS

Make your base. Add strawberries, banana, and almond milk to blender. Blend until smooth, and transfer to a bowl.

Add your toppings. Scatter raspberries and goji berries evenly across surface.

. . . .

VARIATION If you're not in the mood for red, you can also make a super-blue bowl by using frozen blueberries instead of strawberries and adding these toppings:

- ⅛ cup fresh blueberries
- ⅛ cup fresh blackberries

. . . .

RAINBOW BLUEBERRY BOWL

When I need a little cheering up, there's nothing I love more than covering a simple smoothie with tons of colorful toppings. Because this one has so many heavy toppings, the base has to be extra dense. If you're looking for a low-calorie bowl, this isn't it—but I promise it will be delicious, beautiful, and provide you with tons of energy.

Base

1 banana

2 cups frozen blueberries

½ cup almond milk

½ cup cooked oats

Toppings

½ banana, sliced into ½-inch-thick rounds

½ cup strawberries, halved

¼ cup granola

small handful of shredded unsweetened coconut

1 teaspoon chia seeds

INSTRUCTIONS

Make your base. Add banana, blueberries, almond milk, and oats to blender, and blend until smooth. This may take longer than usual, as there's less liquid and more volume. Transfer to a bowl.

Add your toppings. Place toppings in parallel strips: one for banana slices, one for strawberries, one for granola, and one for coconut. Sprinkle chia seeds on top.

. . . .

VARIATION If you want to make this base a little lighter, skip the oats and bananas and let the bowl sit in the freezer for 30 minutes before adding the toppings. When it's slightly frozen, the base will be able to hold the toppings more easily.

. . . .

COCOA AVOCADO BOWL

When I first heard of the avocado-in-a-smoothie concept, I thought it was a bizarre one. But adding half an avocado to a smoothie is a great way to make it creamier, healthier, and add some extra tastiness.

Base

½ avocado

1 banana

1 cup almond milk

1 teaspoon unsweetened cocoa powder

Toppings

½ banana

1 strawberry, sliced

⅛ cup chocolate chips

INSTRUCTIONS

Make your base. Add avocado, banana, almond milk, and cocoa powder to blender, and blend until smooth. Transfer to a bowl.

Add your toppings. Line bowl with banana and strawberry slices, and add chocolate chips to center.

TIP: It can be hard to find ripe avocados (especially in the off season), so buy your avocado a day in advance of making this smoothie and stick it in a paper bag for a day to ripen it more quickly.

CLASSIC ACAI BOWL

I had my first acai bowl in 2007 at a trendy cafe in Santa Cruz, California, and again a few years later in Hawaii. I was blown away each time, so I went on a mission to make my own acai bowls.

Because the acai berry has gotten crazy popular over the past few years thanks to its deliciousness and health benefits (acai berries are packed with antioxidants), frozen acai packs have gotten a lot easier to find in the frozen fruit aisle of local supermarkets. If you're not having any luck, in my experience Whole Foods is always carrying them.

Base

1 frozen unsweetened acai pack

1 banana

1 cup almond milk

1 tablespoon maple syrup

Toppings

½ banana

⅛ cup raspberries

1 tablespoon cacao nibs

1 tablespoon hemp seeds

INSTRUCTIONS

Make your base. Place acai pack, banana, almond milk, and maple syrup in a blender. Blend until smooth, and transfer to a bowl.

Add your toppings. Line bowl with banana and raspberries and place cacao nibs and hemp seeds in the center.

FUN FACT: Acai berries only grow in the rain forest, and they go bad only a day after being picked. For that reason, these tiny berries need to be shipped frozen, which explains why they can be tough to find.

CHERRY BLUEBERRY ALMOND BOWL

Frozen red cherries are easy to find year round. The flavor is tart, the color is bright, and when I add almonds and toss blueberries on top, I'm never disappointed.

Base

1 cup frozen cherries

1 banana

1 cup almond milk

1 tablespoon almond butter

Toppings

¼ cup blueberries

⅛ cup slivered almonds

1 teaspoon honey

INSTRUCTIONS

Make your base. Add frozen cherries, banana, almond milk, and almond butter to blender. Blend until smooth, and transfer to a bowl.

Add your toppings. Line bowl with blueberries and evenly distribute slivered almonds across surface. Drizzle with honey.

VARIATION For a chocolate option, try these toppings:

- ¼ cup blueberries
- ⅛ cup hazelnuts
- ⅛ cup chocolate chips

BIRTHDAY CAKE BOWL

Yes, you can eat a smoothie bowl on your birthday, too. I'm not suggesting you eat one *instead* of cake, but I'm all about waking up with one of these colorful and delicious bowls.

Base

1 frozen banana

1 cup almond milk

1 teaspoon vanilla

1 teaspoon maple syrup

Toppings

½ banana, sliced into ½-inch-thick rounds

1 teaspoon rainbow sprinkles

1 candle

INSTRUCTIONS

Make your base. Add banana, almond milk, vanilla, and maple syrup to blender, and blend until smooth. Transfer to a bowl.

Add your toppings. Pile banana slices on one side of bowl. Spread sprinkles evenly across base and place one banana slice in center. Stick candle in the middle and light at your own risk.

. . . .

VARIATION To make this base taste even more decadent, add:

- 3 dates
- 1 spoonful of almond butter

. . . .

CHOCOLATE CHIP COOKIE BOWL

After ice cream, chocolate chip cookies are my second favorite dessert. Thankfully, it's pretty easy to make a smoothie bowl that tastes a lot like one.

Base

1 frozen banana

1 cup almond milk

1 tablespoon almond butter

3 dates, pitted

Toppings

½ cup chocolate chips

INSTRUCTIONS

Make your base. Add banana, almond milk, almond butter, and dates to blender, and blend until smooth. Transfer to a bowl.

Add your toppings. Evenly distribute chocolate chips across surface of bowl.

TIP: To make this bowl extra flavorful, try adding a few tablespoons of pumpkin puree. If you've ever had a pumpkin chocolate chip cookie, you can probably see why this is a delicious addition.

SUPER STRAWBERRY BOWL

While every berry has its own unique flavor, when I'm getting really crazy with a smoothie bowl, strawberries are a great option because their flavor is a little milder than the flavor of blueberries and raspberries.

Base

1 cup frozen strawberries

1 banana

1 cup almond milk

Toppings

¼ cup blueberries

⅛ cup granola

¼ (1.55-ounce) bar chocolate

1 tablespoon dried goji berries

1 tablespoon cacao nibs

1 teaspoon shredded unsweetened coconut

1 teaspoon chia seeds

INSTRUCTIONS

Make your base. Add strawberries, banana, and almond milk to blender, and blend until smooth. Transfer to a bowl.

Add your toppings. The only rule for toppings is that you have fun—so place the blueberries, granola, chocolate bar pieces, goji berries, cacao nibs, coconut, and chia seeds wherever you'd like.

- -

VARIATION Try these toppings:

- ⅛ cup raspberries
- ⅛ cup blueberries
- ⅛ cup blackberries
- ⅛ cup mango
- 1 teaspoon hemp seeds

BLUEBERRY CLEMENTINE BOWL

Frozen berries are generally available and inexpensive year round, so they make a great base no matter what the season. To make this bowl a bit more wintery, top with sweet clementine slices.

Base

½ cup frozen strawberries

½ cup frozen blueberries

1 banana

1 cup almond milk

Toppings

1 clementine, peeled and broken into slices

1 tablespoon dried goji berries

1 teaspoon cacao nibs

INSTRUCTIONS

Make your base. Add strawberries, blueberries, banana, and almond milk to blender, and blend until smooth. Transfer to a bowl.

Add your toppings. Evenly distribute clementine slices, goji berries, and cacao nibs across bowl.

TIP: Goji berries are one of my all-time favorite smoothie bowl toppings because they're sweet, colorful, nutritious, vaguely spicy, and super crunchy. But if you're using goji berries as a topping, make sure you eat the bowl immediately. Speaking from some very sad experience, tossing your smoothie bowl in the fridge and eating it a few hours later will cause the goji berries to expand and become super mushy.

CRUNCHY BERRY GRANOLA BOWL

Smoothie bowls come in all shapes, sizes, and textures. This one is extremely crunchy, sweet, and flavorful. It's basically the smoothie version of a bowl of cereal.

Base

1 frozen banana

1 cup almond milk

1 teaspoon vanilla

1 teaspoon ground cinnamon

Toppings

⅛ cup blueberries

⅛ cup raspberries

¾ cup granola

⅛ cup chocolate chips

INSTRUCTIONS

Make your base. Add banana, almond milk, vanilla, and cinnamon to blender, and blend until smooth. Transfer to a bowl.

Add your toppings. Heap blueberries, raspberries, granola, and chocolate chips on top.

VARIATION For an even crunchier bowl, try these toppings:

- ¾ cup granola
- 1 teaspoon chia seeds
- 1 teaspoon hemp seeds
- 1 tablespoon dried goji berries

CHOCOLATE PEANUT BUTTER ICE CREAM SUNDAE BOWL

Did the title fool you? Good, because you can probably fool yourself (and anyone else) into thinking this creamy delight is chocolate peanut butter ice cream.

Base

1 frozen banana

½ avocado

1 cup almond milk

1 teaspoon maple syrup

1 tablespoon unsweetened cocoa powder

Toppings

1 tablespoon peanut butter

1 strawberry

¼ cup chocolate chips

INSTRUCTIONS

Make your base. Add banana, avocado, almond milk, maple syrup, and cocoa powder to blender, and blend until smooth. Transfer to a bowl.

Add your toppings. Mix in peanut butter and place strawberry on top, then microwave chocolate chips until totally melted (this should take a minute or less), and pour over smoothie like chocolate syrup.

- -

VARIATION For a twist on this bowl, try these toppings:

- ⅛ cup chopped peanuts
- ⅛ cup chopped almonds
- 1 cherry
- ¼ cup chocolate chips, melted

- -

BANANA SPLIT BOWL

As you've probably noticed by now, I'll jump at any chance to make my smoothie look (and taste) like ice cream, and this bowl is no exception. Dare I say it's *better* than a classic banana split?!

Base

1 frozen banana

1 cup almond milk

1 teaspoon maple syrup

1 tablespoon unsweetened cocoa powder

Toppings

1 banana, sliced in half

2 strawberries

⅛ cup raspberries

⅛ cup blueberries

⅛ cup cashews

INSTRUCTIONS

Make your base. Add banana, almond milk, maple syrup, and cocoa to blender, and blend until smooth. Transfer to a bowl.

Add your toppings. Place sliced banana on either side of bowl, and add strawberries, raspberries, blueberries, and cashews to center.

VARIATION Need more chocolate? Try these toppings:

- 1 banana, sliced in half
- 2 cherries
- ⅛ cup chopped almonds
- ⅛ cup chocolate chips, melted

STRAWBERRY PEANUT BUTTER SMOOTHIE

When I was a kid, I was obsessed with a smoothie shop near my house that did something unheard of back before smoothies were trendy: They added peanut butter to my smoothies. All of my friends thought it was disgusting, but I couldn't get enough of it. Once I got my own blender, the first thing I did was make one of these creamy, nutty smoothies.

Base

1 cup frozen strawberries

1 banana

1 tablespoon peanut butter

1 cup almond milk

Toppings

⅛ cup chopped strawberries

⅛ cup blueberries

⅛ cup chocolate chips

⅛ cup granola

1 teaspoon shredded unsweetened coconut

INSTRUCTIONS

Make your base. Add strawberries, banana, peanut butter, and almond milk to blender, and blend until smooth. Transfer to a bowl.

Add your toppings. Line one side of bowl with strawberries and the other with blueberries, and pile chocolate chips, granola, and coconut in center.

. . . .

VARIATION If the peanut butter flavor is too strong for you, try using other nut butters like almond butter or cashew butter. If you don't want to buy an entire jar, toss in any kind of nuts you have on hand. If your blender is powerful enough, they should blend in easily.

. . . .

LIGHT
Bowls

Although they tend to be on the healthier side of breakfasts, sometimes the calories in smoothie bowls can seriously add up when nuts get involved. In this section, you'll find bowls that are 350 calories or less—a good option when you're trying to keep things on the lighter side.

COCONUT BLUEBERRY BOWL

TOTAL CALORIES: 270

While coconut *can* tack on a ton of calories (while making any smoothie bowl even tastier), this is a way to add coconut to your smoothie and keep it low calorie.

Base

1 cup frozen blueberries

½ banana

1 cup almond milk

Toppings

⅛ cup pineapple

⅛ cup blueberries

⅛ cup blackberries

⅛ cup strawberries

1 tablespoon shredded unsweetened coconut

INSTRUCTIONS

Make your base. Add frozen blueberries, banana, and almond milk to blender, and blend until smooth. Transfer to a bowl.

Add your toppings. Add pineapple and blueberries to one side and blackberries and strawberries to other side. Add coconut to center.

· ·

VARIATION If you love the flavor of coconut, you can get even more of that without adding calories by using coconut milk (the kind that comes in a box, not a can) instead of almond milk. The calorie count is usually about the same.

· ·

THE HEALTHIEST SMOOTHIE BOWL EVER

TOTAL CALORIES: 330

A bold statement, I know. But this one is packed with vegetables, antioxidants, and healthy fats, and also happens to be delicious.

Base

1 banana

½ cup kale

1 cup spinach

1 cup almond milk

1 tablespoon almond butter

Toppings

¼ cup blueberries

¼ cup blackberries

INSTRUCTIONS

Make your base. Add banana, kale, spinach, almond milk, and almond butter to blender, and blend until smooth. Transfer to a bowl.

Add your toppings. Evenly distribute blueberries and blackberries across surface of bowl.

TIP: To make this one even healthier, try slicing up a bit of fresh ginger and tossing it in your blender. Ginger is great for both digestion and calming an upset stomach.

BLUEBERRY WATERMELON KIWI BOWL

TOTAL CALORIES: 185

The key to keeping a smoothie bowl light is avoiding foods like nuts and seeds (while healthy, coconut and avocado are big offenders as they're high in calories). So pile on the fruit! This one is so low calorie that it can be eaten as a snack.

Base

1 cup frozen blueberries

1 cup almond milk

Toppings

½ cup chopped watermelon

1 kiwi, sliced

INSTRUCTIONS

Make your base. Add frozen blueberries and almond milk to blender, and blend until smooth. Transfer to a bowl.

Add your toppings. Add kiwi to one side and watermelon to opposite side.

VARIATION For a less sugary (and higher-calorie) version of this bowl, try these toppings:

- ½ banana, sliced into ½-inch-thick rounds
- 1 tablespoon cacao nibs
- 1 tablespoon shredded unsweetened coconut
- 1 teaspoon chia seeds
- 1 teaspoon hemp seeds

MANGO MINT BOWL

TOTAL CALORIES: 250

Mango and mint go together like peanut butter and jelly (or something like that). Heap some fruit on top and you've got a creamy, sweet, low-calorie bowl.

Base

1 cup frozen mango

1 cup almond milk

Toppings

3 mint leaves

¼ banana, sliced into ½-inch-thick rounds

⅛ cup blueberries

⅛ cup raspberries

⅛ cup mango

INSTRUCTIONS

Make your base. Add mango and almond milk to blender, and blend until smooth. Transfer to a bowl.

Add your toppings. Line one side with mint leaves and the other with bananas. Add blueberries, raspberries, and mango to center.

TIP: If you want to add a little kick to this bowl, add the juice of half a lemon to the base. A little bit of tartness can go a long way.

MANGO GREEN SMOOTHIE BOWL

TOTAL CALORIES: 340

This one tastes like summer and is a great go-to when you're trying to keep your breakfast light and your flavor strong.

Base

1 banana

¾ cup frozen mango

1 cup almond milk

2 cups spinach

Toppings

⅛ cup granola

INSTRUCTIONS

Make your base. Add banana, frozen mango, almond milk, and spinach to blender. Blend until smooth, and transfer to a bowl.

Add your topping. Sprinkle granola evenly on top.

· ·

VARIATION For a colorful twist on this bowl, try these toppings:

- ⅛ cup raspberries
- ⅛ cup blueberries
- ⅛ cup mango
- 1 teaspoon shredded unsweetened coconut

· ·

BLUEBERRY BANANA BOWL

TOTAL CALORIES: 276

Blueberries and bananas are a magical, satisfying, low-calorie combination. It's hard to not get on board with this one.

Base

1 ½ cups frozen blueberries

1 cup almond milk

Toppings

½ banana, sliced into ½-inch-thick rounds

½ cup raspberries

½ cup blueberries

INSTRUCTIONS

Make your base. Add blueberries and almond milk to blender, and blend until smooth. Transfer to a bowl.

Add your toppings. Line bowl with bananas and evenly distribute raspberries and blueberries across surface.

TIP: Adding 1 tablespoon of peanut butter to the base of this bowl will tack on just 100 calories and add tons of flavor and deliciousness.

STRAWBERRY MINT BASIL BOWL

TOTAL CALORIES: 190

When you're craving a smoothie that tastes fresh and healthy, this bowl is the way to go. Your taste buds will explode, I promise.

Base

1 cup frozen strawberries

½ banana

1 cup almond milk

1 teaspoon vanilla

⅛ cup chopped basil

Toppings

1 strawberry, sliced

2 mint leaves

½ banana, sliced into ½-inch-thick rounds

2 basil leaves

INSTRUCTIONS

Make your base. Add strawberries, banana, almond milk, vanilla, and basil to blender, and blend until smooth. Transfer to a bowl.

Add your toppings. Line one side of bowl with strawberry slices and the other with mint leaves, and add stripes of banana slices and basil to center.

VARIATION Don't like mint? Try these toppings:

- ⅛ cup blueberries
- ⅛ cup raspberries
- ½ banana, sliced into ½-inch-thick rounds

BLUEBERRY LIME BOWL

TOTAL CALORIES: 240

This bowl is super refreshing, delicious, and low in calories. And the whole lime factor might even trick you into thinking you're drinking a margarita for breakfast.

Base

1 cup frozen blueberries

1 cup almond milk

juice from ½ lime

Toppings

¼ cup blueberries

½ banana, sliced into 1-inch-thick rounds

1 lime, cut into half-moon slices

INSTRUCTIONS

Make your base. Add blueberries, almond milk, and lime juice to blender, and blend until smooth. Transfer to a bowl.

Add your toppings. Evenly distribute blueberries, banana, and lime slices on surface of bowl.

FUN FACT: If you think the only thing limes are good for is chasing tequila shots, think again. Studies have shown that limes also aid with weight loss and improve digestion.

SWEET AND SOUR BLACKBERRY BOWL

TOTAL CALORIES: 350

Blackberries have a rich color and a distinct flavor, and can either be super sweet, super sour, or a little bit of both, which is why I call this one the sweet and sour blackberry bowl.

Base

1 banana

1 cup frozen blackberries

1 cup almond milk

Toppings

¼ cup fresh raspberries

¼ cup blueberries

¼ cup granola

INSTRUCTIONS

Make your base. Add banana, blackberries, and almond milk to blender, and blend until smooth. Transfer to a bowl.

Add your toppings. Line bowl with raspberries and blueberries, and add mountain of granola to center.

. . . .

VARIATION If you can't find frozen blackberries at the store, frozen cherries are just as delicious and have that same tartness.

. . . .

CHOCOLATE MILK BOWL

TOTAL CALORIES: 340

There's a reason I add so much chocolate to my smoothies: It's actually kind of healthy (it's full of antioxidants, and studies show that chocolate eaters are happier), and when eaten in a specific way, it can also be low in calories. While I prefer to mix my chocolate with peanut butter, this is a great go-to when you're trying to keep things on the lighter side.

Base

1 frozen banana

½ tablespoon almond butter

1 cup almond milk

Toppings

½ banana

1 tablespoon chocolate chips

INSTRUCTIONS

Make your base. Add banana, almond butter, and almond milk to blender, and blend until smooth. Transfer to a bowl.

Add your toppings. Line bowl with banana and chocolate chips.

TIP: To make this one extra chocolaty (and pile on the health benefits), look for dark chocolate chips that are made up of at least 70 percent cocoa.

MEAN GREEN BOWL

TOTAL CALORIES: 250

There's no doubt about it: Green smoothies have an intimidating look to them. But adding greens to your smoothie does almost nothing to the bowl's overall flavor, and it's a great way to get your nutrients in first thing in the morning. This one has a fresh, sweet, and slightly sour taste.

Base

1 banana

1 cup spinach

½ cup kale

1 cup almond milk

Toppings

1 kiwi, sliced into half moons

3 basil leaves

3 mint leaves

INSTRUCTIONS

Make your base. Add banana, spinach, kale, and almond milk to blender, and blend until smooth. Transfer to a bowl.

Add your toppings. Evenly distribute kiwi slices, basil leaves, and mint leaves across surface.

- -

VARIATION Try these toppings instead:

- 1 apple, sliced into chunks
- ½ kiwi, sliced into half moons
- 1 tablespoon dried goji berries

- -

CONCLUSION

If you've made it this far, I'm assuming you've whipped up some of my creations as well as some of your own. Good for you!

But don't let your smoothie bowl journey end here. I encourage you to keep experimenting with new combinations and toppings because you never know when you'll happen upon the most delicious smoothie bowl that makes you feel awesome all day long.

While there's no doubt that smoothie bowls are beautiful, don't lose sight of the most important thing about them: When done right, they're really, really good for you.

And if you burn out on smoothie bowls or don't feel like having them in the winter when it's freezing out (I've been there), when it comes to breakfast there are tons of super-nutritious and easy things you can do.

Try making oatmeal in your slow cooker. Try tossing it in a mason jar with some coconut milk, chia seeds, and a banana, and letting it soak overnight. Try making a batch of quinoa on your stove and mixing in almond butter, berries, and hemp seeds. For a super-easy, fibrous breakfast that will keep you full past lunch, try putting 2 tablespoons of chia seeds in a mason jar with almond milk and maple syrup before you go to bed.

While eating a delicious breakfast is fun, I hope your main takeaway from this book is that eating a breakfast packed with nutrients is crazy important when it comes to your overall health. The energy you get in the morning is essential to your performance at work, your workouts, and how you interact with others.

So I hope you make a habit out of packing your morning with vegetables, protein, fat, and fruit. It will make your day—and life—so much better.

ACKNOWLEDGMENTS

First and foremost, I'd like to thank my insanely talented coworker and friend Celine Rahman, who took every photograph in this book. Celine, thank you for hopping on board with this project and believing in it from the moment I brought it up to you. Your creativity, positive attitude, and patience throughout this entire process made it so much more fun. It is such a privilege to know you.

Thanks to everyone at Elite Daily for cheering me on, supporting me, and getting behind this project. Thanks to Kourtney Joy and Casie Vogel at Ulysses Press for stalking me on Instagram and asking me to write this book in the first place. You were both tremendously helpful throughout this entire process!

To my sister Brenna: I'm not sure how I would have navigated this project or the many before it without your support, advice, and knack for knowing exactly when I need some sense knocked into me.

To my parents, Mary and Cliff, who bought me a blender three years ago when I was completely broke, because I somehow convinced them that I "really, really needed it." See? I was right! Thanks for always being so proud of me for being creative even though I was terrible at math and science. You're the best parents.

To everyone in my enormous family, especially Grandma Doris. Thank you for thinking I am so famous and telling all of your friends that I am.

To my loyal, hilarious, and amazing friends, particularly Reika McCracken, Tanya Swartz, Tulani Weeks, Cara Patton, Kiki Von Glinow, Jessie Heyman, Emily Laurence, Jordan Zakarin, Rikki Bahar, and Catherine Taibi—you are all truly the best.

And an enormous thanks to the guy I love most in the world, Michael Klopman. Thanks for the endless love, support, laughter, Instagram filter advice, and always telling people that you "can't even taste the kale." I adore you!

ABOUT THE AUTHOR

Leigh Weingus is a writer and editor living in New York City. When she's not testing out new recipes and dissecting the latest health trends, she's checking out a new yoga studio, Instagramming fruit and vegetables, in a really long line at Trader Joe's, or holding plank for a torturous two minutes in the name of strengthening her core. Originally from Oakland, California, Leigh graduated from the University of California, Davis, in 2009, and has since worked as a writer and editor at *The Huffington Post*, *Elite Daily*, and *J-14 Magazine*.